LOVE AND/IN POETRY

LOVE AND/IN POETRY

WRITTEN BY

Jhonny B. Pierre

authorHOUSE®

AuthorHouse™
1663 Liberty Drive
Bloomington, IN 47403
www.authorhouse.com
Phone: 1-800-839-8640

Published by AuthorHouse   02/06/2013

ISBN: 978-1-4772-8637-1 (sc)
ISBN: 978-1-4817-0764-0 (e)

CONTENTS

INTRODUCTION

This book is a sample, and a foretaste. It is the description of true love manifested in human kind to express toward each other the sensation within.

To my concern, it started a few years back in college at Florida Atlantic University, FAU, as a member of a student club organization by the name of Konbit Kreyol (KK) jointing during key events with Black Students Association (BSU) in the years between 2001 and 2005. BSU had provided a poetry club for students to express their words and their talents. From then, I was inspired by the energy it supplied to a person; it also served as a catalyst to make shine the true feeling burning within me.

I started writing just for fun one after another, but never realized that it would develop in me to be rather part of me. A few years later, I decided to be more serious about expressing my voice through my words. My first few poems were written about the view of women in our lives. As I was always a strong advocate for women, I started to express my affection toward them in every aspect I could think of, especially love at intimacy, my mother, and so on. I wrote my first serious poem back in 2006 and 2007; then on I continued, and become attached about two years later.

Earlier this year (2012), I also got inspired by reading poetry books to increase my ideas which truly helped me in sorting out all my emotions in a more suitable manner.

As the title is *Love and/in Poetry*, I am certain that you, the reader, will be filled with satisfaction in reading these love based poems. As I present to you the true inner side of me, I want you to treasure these thoughts and try to use them in your daily endeavors by actions and/or by words to help in the process of making this word safer and more livable.

A Beautiful Woman-

How beautiful is such a creature!
A certain morning arose;
The clouds are already in such a beautiful pattern to complement with an atmosphere so comfortable.
The happiness of all the flowers for a new life of solar energy appears with a smooth wind that blows with enough power just enough to open the flowers to release an incredible odor.

The birds are singing in harmony all different songs, but with the same purpose of a new day from heaven.
Beside all these characters, what else can be more beautiful that is part of this vast and admirable nature? Damn! I need to know . . . .

As the sun is still low,
and the shades are extended enough to make a highway, but among all these miracles that may seem to be a routine of this great mother land, something from far seems to bother my eyes and seems to be more beautiful and more important of all.

Spontaneously, I thought, this must be an angel from God;
And I suddenly recognized strongly from that moment that I was already in paradise.
My heart was pounded with a normal chest movement while only an elephant could be as strong at that point to push the blood through my veins.
I didn't waste any time, I approached her with a smile on my face.
Her beautiful smile and the sheet of beauty covering her whole-self shine the light in my face
And I immediately know that this special creature, an Angel, is DEFINITELY "YOU"

A mother's love

Once upon a time within the universe
Certainly with the approval of the Highest
It's quite similar to the Arc angel, Gabriel
A rational decision was made
Then all because of me, a sin was then exonerated

In times of preparation, thousands of ideas come to mind
If it's a girl, she'd be my Nubian queen
And of course, a boy would be my prince charming
Excited but not even knowing if your man would mind
And geared up to commit to a day foreseen

Harsh by the day itself now comes times for consequences
From the height of your beauty now thousands of body changes
Presented as breast augmentation
Followed by super size pieces such as lips, feet and especially the
tummy
Nine months to commit to was certainly something to worry

As you're prepared to deliver
Here I was ready to face earth
Kicking and punching and even rolling around
Diving upside down with a pain mild and greater
While I demanded out so I could experience my first breath

Yes here I am; so thank you mom and dad
Tiny and helpless but that did not make you sad
Before and after every blink, you were there
Spoiled by your eyes, I found ways to cry
Unable to understand why, but you still gave it a try

I, eating by the hour, so feeding was hard
Picky as I was, but your selection was trusted
To the level of my inexperience, I ate then I vomited
Without teeth I ate until I was full
With weak mastication, then on you I drooled

Devoted for my well being,
You coped with high level of patience.
From you I learned manners for a normal living.
Without words to speak, still I was amused by your exchange
Cause chatting without understanding could not be more motivating

Also on my first steps you were there
To hold me and serve as my personal protector
Morning and later, you took me in and out of day care
Besides all the responsibilities, you sustained as an excellent provider
Now with the experience I obtained was because you cared

As time elapsed also did my transformation gradually
Eight point six pounds was great, then better at forty
Morning and night you never left my sight
With confidence and encouragement, real tall I stand
Because of your broad shoulders, my process was brilliant

Well prepared for the world, I am
Through knocks and destitution, I persevered
After years of your determination, you are who I am
By your love and commitment, it's a job well deserved
I'm grateful to you and your teaching will never lam

Thank you mother
Your blessing will come from the almighty Father
If it was my choice of life
I would wish you that you live forever
As you showed me the pattern to shine so bright

A thought of the moments that have gone by
It's unattainable to repay you for the mother of your kind
Despite of your constructive character, you are beautiful in heart
Understanding your struggles, yet I am grateful
And from being a toddler to my presence, I thank you

A real Man's dream

From the eye balls to the brain perceived images based on individual judgment
Often enough it is the image of an opinion relevant
Accompanied by chances, it's the appearance that causes Eurasian wryneck
A look that dominates a man's ego; sounds foolish, but what the heck

Therefore, a real man's dream . . . is the one who can talk to impress
        One that attracts attention in every word
          Fully acknowledgeable of issues by using the right verb
          The one requires concentration only by her lips in progress

In every culture a woman's feature is based on her racial genetic make-up
Some lacking a trait, but another as a genetic make-over
Lucky if you may, it's the features of a devilish cherub
That bring light to the opposite sex while the soul is been taken over

Therefore, a real man's dream . . . is the one who can walk and makes others eyes hurt
          One who twists like a snake but maintains in the same plan
          One who brings fear by demonstrating her self-worth
          A walk to kill or to illustrate pride as a mental punishment

As much as we pretend, no one is more beautiful than one with quality of a good character
She may not be appealing in the outside but has a big heart to conquer
Civilization may diverge, but beauty is truly a bonus while character is a gift
As genetically formulated or later develop as a blessing

Therefore, a real man's dream . . . is the one who brings so much laughter
          Very outgoing and has a cheerful nature
          One with a sincere personality that melts
          Also a character with friendship to collect

Jhonny B. Pierre

Hideous or not, someone with bad etiquettes is water to a fire
An overview of such matter brings back-flashes to a future wretchedly
A woman respectful with good manners to capture
Very understanding and values the purpose of life accordingly

Therefore, a real man's dream . . . is the one who respects her own values
            And understands relationship details instead of her own self
            One who's self-educated, and will cause no harm in public
            One who obeys principles for the merit of the great of good

Generally speaking, love is eternal only where quality care is giving
As been said, domestic training leads to obedience by a common love to offer
True love comes with care deeply from the heart with zilch to cover
Like a two-way street or a parallel tube equally engaging

Therefore, a real man's dream . . . is someone who cares instead of an opportunity taker
            One who believes in love instead of a moment of pleasure
            One with limited jalousie and able to properly fall in love
            One who treats me right according to the One above

According to the human nature, life is perfect due to the fact that it's imperfect
The behavior of the planet sometimes is destructive but perhaps misunderstood
Thus someone with a loud behavior is not necessarily dreadful instead viewed incorrect
Someone with a soothing behavior is one who has proper control of whatever the mood

Therefore, a real man's dream . . . is the one with a behavior to endure
            One who behaves like a queen fully allured
            Who conducts herself suitably while sometimes silly
            And studies my behavior and tempers justice with mercy

Free of addiction, still we each have something we crave for
As understanding our nature is a mystery or it's best viewed as metaphor
A strong family is one well maintained by an excellent woman
A woman with inherited principles not lacking confidence

Therefore, a real man's dream . . . is the one who can lead with complete affection
One that makes her presence reign
Who embraces life with full intuition
Someone to die for and ready to ordain

As it normally mention that a man's best companion is his dog
But believe it or not, a real man's best friend is undeniably his woman
Someone who subsist life with great influence
A woman with ambition and respect for the Lord

Therefore, a real man's dream . . . is someone who values commitment
One who invests in spending time together
One who invests in our future forever
One who is a friend to affix to and has good judgment

Based on what I experience, you are absolutely the woman of my preference
Totally for your great values
And as my dream . . . . Come true!!!

Commitment scare

Three months to one year of satisfaction may have been a practice
Full of purpose while life is young and feel like an entire generation
Deeply in love and much skills to learn as an obedient apprentice
Comes the understanding of worship from a heart of imperfection
Therefore; If the lawn is green
Then the mower must as well be near

As the days still immature so appears my life in full velocity
Totally attached as a magnet my soul must already reach in heaven
Kisses in abundance which require not a moment to insist
But being appraised on a regular basis gives me the pride of a gentleman

As times elapsed the soul befalls to intensely in love
Contented is my mate and got more comfortable with my genres
Solemn is a mockery as we comprehend things by role
We also acknowledge the pains required, higher than a full fence
Then minstrels woke within me
As rose is been portrayed to win me
My mind is blind and my vision is no where far
Nothing at this point is controlled
While my dream evaded the skull in a space happily dark
This reached the level as love's ultimate threshold

Wonderful as its been then comes room for sober
A heart so fragile that was once my life enrichment
Escalate to the heights that such feeling upholds room for temper
Life is a game and its players must be gamed to be viewed as amusement

The days shrink in sizes then yet it grimes
Although my attitude reaches something to climb
Times go by, then interest falls to the market

My investment assured, but the attention slopes to the negative
Loss of appetite is fair with a complete loss of respect
In fact, it's the process of maturity as one love's electives

Like the day advances, then the night is at its early appearance
A storm is near as the cloud took over
Also my focus is troubled by love's true existence
To the altitude of occurrence of a heart switched over
Never in mind for a time so right
To realize the shift of affection to the far right
Absorbing the bumps it appeared somehow appalling
Based on the behavior already shown make me question a few years ahead
Optimistic is wise only with proper planning
Overwhelmed and bewildered of course I turn pale

Painful as it seems my dream can't be real
A future plain and tiresome, I would rather stay at home
A life so miserable has no place in a streak
With whom I'm devoted not to ever be alone
Living is precious and to us it's a grace
Where our behavior is selfish and fully out of place

Twisted inside will I still be the one when things forever gone?
Unthinkable is the future for the shrine of a heart without fate
And pressure sums up by the judgment of right or wrong
Aloud as a silent killer my heart has to expatriate

More bemused I become I remain well connected
Derailed by character but at ease is my future
My mind is set to a feeling tightly bonded
My craving in crescendo makes the spotlight to configure
Sometimes in life, a moment so weak
Can't be any more right to realize the spikes at your feet

Jhonny B. Pierre

Despite all my abhors I am here to stay
Occasions of one another I'm insulted, verbally or physically abused
But deep to the core our love is my foreplay
My affection forward is guaranteed like super glue

As experience matured then my reality has mustered
Everything is a recycle while love is no exception
My adoration lingers with feelings still retired
Clear as H2O and ready for lifetime duration

It is no gimmick in nature even to what seems marvelous
Like beauty is temporary to the distance short and obvious
Being knowledgeable of our differences I accept my knocks
Ready to move on I come to my bow
Life is a well-organized challenge with tons to flock
Thus for now and forward my commitment remains on the row

Cuddling

Beautiful is the sunny day with a mild temperature very comfortable
My day is as easy as it could, and the mood is nothing less than something
    relaxable
It can't feel any better than a moment so perfect
It must be the right moment to feel in love knowing that I am imperfect

Despite the most enjoyable trice,
here comes the love of my life
I jumped up and offer the tightest capable hug with all my teeth embedded in
    a smile
A smile so bright
That clarifies all the affection types
Starring at the opposite big eyes in front of mines,
my face has vocalized its kind
The behavior in reciprocity is just enough to be recognized

Changing from work attire and now in a moment of full desire
It must be abnormal that my circulation is speeding and my blood is on fire
Looking at the way my baby is created I wonder if my eyes suddenly become
    a laser scanner
To accommodate in response, I decide to make myself vulnerable and not be a
    complainer

As usual, no one has a better place in my heart than the one I love
We typically act a foul but still have the bond that only seen in a pair of
    doves
We know each other so well, and that definitely puts my mind at ease
Usually addresses me so gentle and soft, I am normally melted like I was
    American cheese
We totally care for each other and that just blows my mind
My words are carefully chosen and resulted in two hearts in love combined

So much is already said by just involving in full eye contact
At that split second I must have developed some wings since my feet had lost
     ground contact
Going further, the hips movements are self-explanatory
The chest pumping is well simulated that my heart movement demarcates
     away from my respiratory
One of us is completely in pink
While the outfit of the other is something to make you think

The facial expression received is greater than words
The smile on my face makes me bark like a dog but obedient like a German
     shepherd
As silent words take over, we find ourselves speechless but totally loud in
     mind
I take advantage of the moment, and leave no regrets behind
From the opposite eyes, the future is clear, detailing a full story in a simple
     wink
While a whole world of adventure appears in a plain blink

We fell in a moment rich of desire
Despite of the adrenaline, we become slow while the silent got higher
With all that may be expected, we probably just started a bonfire
Coming out of my boundaries, you are really the one that I admire

The longer is the moment, the more the situation got intense
We end up on the couch, leaning on each other while utterly content
A back, and neck massage is great
Thus my hands at work is a grace
My palm so soft and gentle
Entirely opposite to a work out in the huddle

It feels so right and as we are now on the same page
Our body is trembling which may seem like we're acting in rage
With my hands going through the skin

I realize everything that is there to know by a single hint
My sub-dermal nerves find times to feel the bumps in its sum
In which I come to understand the shape of a goose bump

Never tempting to slow down
Instead become a moment of show down
It has never been a better time than this to increase the air condition
But no one has the courage to get up as we are completely in exhaustion
It may be the right time to call for termination
As an alternative, we fall in more determination

As times elapse, we must be going out of control
But among us two, who has the right mind to recall?
We seem to take it all the way to the finish line as we feel more connection
This then, leads us to a period of chaste admiration
The time is going and no one is counting down
If I may speak for both of us, we are nowhere near of letting down

Rushing to the emotion inside
We still find patient to deliver and mollify
As we gradually came down to slow speed
We find ourselves with the lips soft and dry in a position of coddling
As our temperature begins to drop, we realize also that we were watching
    television
At this era we are already full of satisfaction
Yet, it's already three in the morning
It seems that we are fully awaken
As the new day is very young
We look at each other and recognize that we were far beyond

Daddy's Greatness!!

From the time of my reconnaissance, you've been my dad
Growing within your boundaries is precious, and for which I'm
glad
A man of your words
As well as honest to the world
Someone with a great character
As you teach life with such moral fiber

Your presence is amusing
As your zest for life is my everyday craving
Unthinkable are your jokes with a smile on your face
Is my red bull to revive my frantic day.
Your existence in the house brings heat and affection
Which, is comparably to a house full of illumination

Never fail to commit and stand to life's provision
In hard work and through the process of life as a lesson
Grinding and jostling, you stood up with courage
Understanding your responsibilities, you made me your fate
You're the man in the morning
As much as the man in the evening

A home without God is a place missing peace
While the house without you in it, is definitely missing a piece
You are the pole of the corners
As well as every one's protector
With comfort and toughness
Your umbrella does remain priceless

For the father that you are, I love you
For your presence around me, I appreciate you
A father of compassion, and with great patience
Someone respectful with ample resilience
For your presence in my good and time of need,
You're my fortress and I love you dearly

Flashback on Valentine's Day

Unh . . . unh . . . unh, what a day . . . what a day . . . need I say
  more?
A day we accept to consider love without war
A day to show love without cause
A day to give thanks in the name of love
In many cases, a day to just love for God's sake
But without our action fully fake
A day where to accept others for their best
By telling others that you're really suck but today you're blessed
Just thinking of such a day
I have to say that on this date, you make my day

Everything from the past need to be forgotten and celebrated on the
  day of Valentine
However, do you have an idea who is Saint Valentine?
By looking at your face, today you feel content
But I thought you don't believe in saints?
He was a loving man and very expressive about marriage
So this day was adopted to commemorate his courage
Have we fêted the day to the height of its purpose?
Or we have lost the idea and make it based on our own interest?
Let's use this current time and think for a moment
For some, it is a date to show commitment
For others, it is a day to feel good while in the moment
As we tend to forget our past to make it a celebration so brilliant

How can we spend so much time fighting?
And today you are nothing but my precious darling?
Times after times it seemed like I was transparent and see right
  through me
But today, I become your focus like radar guided
Throughout the year, how many times you cause me pain

But only today I become your admirable friend
Usually when I spoke my words made no sense
Today I suddenly become your positive influence

I usually hear day after day how much I look dreadful
Since this morning, all I've been hearing is that I am beautiful
My face is never good enough no matter how I fixed it up
And I am already told today how much you love me even without my
    make-up

Quite often I'm lectured of how much I've gain weight
But today I was asked "have you lost some weight"?
When I ask for something, the response is usually "it's over here
    when you need it"
Instead, I was served and told that "I'll get it for you, just ask if
    you ever need it"

In the morning, I wake up fixing the side of your bed without your
    presence
Today, I woke up with your legs on my waist, and start thinking if
    that is your horse sense
My morning greeting is normally from far, as it always seemed as
    you are in a rush
But today, I was surprised with a moist kiss on my lips and that got
    me blushed

What I eat was never your concern
But today, we spent time on discussing healthy food that will keep me
    firm
When the meal is ready, I usually eat and save your plate like I am
    feeding an invisible monster
But today, I was getting help to eat like a baby who is still on
    Gerber
It is always my duty to know that when you come home your food will
    be there

Today, not only you were there, but I was told which place we will
    spend time and have dinner
Normally we talk, discuss and argue about things just to get the day
    going
But today, I have time to admire your denture and your dimples while
    looking at you smiling

When I'm getting dressed, you always in a rush to leave me and
    wonder if I'll ever be ready
But today, you have notice my shape with so much dinky donkey
For you, my blouse is always fixed the wrong way and wonder if a
    button is always missing
But today you notice my cups with your eyes wondering
My legs are so strong that you comment sometimes that they shape
    like a man
But today you offered to put lotion for me with your strong hands
When I complain to have more time together, you always respond that
    your life is a hustle
But today you have all the time in the world to cuddle

But I see, you really think you slick
Tell me the truth, you want me to be your freak
As today is special, I'm not complaining
I just want to make sure that we have the same understanding

As the evening is still young,
I like all the attention you have shown
Therefore, happy valentine's day; I love you and I love your
    cooperation
But for today, you will not get in my provision . . .
Good Night
And Happy Valentine's!!!

Her perfect gentleman

From the moon to the human planet
We differentiate on character
Docile and tender to the extent I appreciate
Difficult and paltry we express disgrace
Down to earth is the winner at least for God's sake
Passionate and concern my soul will relate

A planer all around very much separated from a condenser
A mind full of thoughts where dreams in numbers generate
Occupied by seconds usually result in great behavior
Optimistic and courageous is a bonus to this stretched race
Bright future oriented with love deeply adopted
An analyzer of the past with tomorrow's vivid hope
Who measures frequently with the motives well anticipated
An appraiser of sufferings for the greatness of vital goals

A robust appearance that perceives passion by tender feeling
A Resemblance of my divine guardian with uplifted spirit
In a posture gigantic with the unconditional swagger
With large body parts including the unrestricted factor
Well maintained and deserve undivided attention
An eye popping stature with guilt sufficient to invoke temptation

A master in composure with features deadly gorgeous
A devil smile to baffle the soul concatenating pleasure
With the stare that kills with features extremely contagious
Eyes of an eagle confiscating interest as a heavenly creature
Physical appearance frankly adorable
With a pounding pulse of admiration to an essence insane
The chest of a horse tall as an admiral
Representing a compact feature embedded with an affection ordained

Jhonny B. Pierre

One with an attachment full of desire
A kind that matters while internally on fire
A degree so resistible but in a jam-packed strength of resilience
Ready to settle while in mind I will find residence
A respectable contender as well as an investor in sacrifice
For the pride in sagacity inherited and self-defined

To thee my heart burns
Desperate and agitated, I should surrender
Content and fulfilled but definitely self-assured
With true love onsite to remain my heart beholder
Perhaps one with the size so minute
But the heart of equivalent colossal elephant
A believer with ample love to compute
Not a character, but my ideal motivation toward pure romance

I'm falling . . .

On a peaceful afternoon walking down the street
Laid-back or to the pace of others enjoying a moment rather passive
Thinking of all my necessary toils
The time could not be any better to escape my troubles
In my hands found my mobile device
Newly purchased, with my fingers enjoying my mobile apps
Accidently dropped it on the ground
Then heartbroken by such a mistake, but full of attention in the background

From the ground going up
A change of my attention has terrifically built up
Impressively moving is the appearance of a mobile mass
Half a mile away which is relatively far
But I become totally in shock by the shape of its shadow
As I can't craft a face, then is my instinct to follow
Trying to recover, I am now beat up
By the observation of such an incredible walk

As I'm stepping forward
The moment is getting further awkward
I am baffled by the appealing style
Existing in such a body dancing to an odd rhyme
Caressing each move while embodied in an exceptional beauty
I suddenly wipe my face wondering if I was not in a dream
Confused to the reality, my soul dropped by such body language
As I'm fighting for strength at that moment, my heart gets entirely engaged

Besides everything I just encounter
It's insane that there's more to proffer
Trembling in my skin, but manage to introduce myself in a weak chorus
Then, my pulse instantly disappeared to the sound of such beautiful voice

Shaky are my hands and my legs unstable by such a beautiful character
I got humbled and became a stunning epicure
I could not resist listening to such a vocal cord with supreme softness
Which puts me in an instantaneous total weakness.

Impressively speechless by someone with such incredible attitude
My existence must be appreciated with lofty gratitude
Smiling and engaging in my conversation, my words lost its composition
To me, it's more or less a moment of delusion
Very affable and interesting to talk to
My ears dance with my attention getting more heedful
Extraordinarily acknowledgeable, and very open-minded
How regretful would I be if that moment never existed?

With my eyes wide open, it's empirical to recognize a body so impeccable
Thus, I lose track of myself to someone so adorable
My stomach is bothered while my heart beat is excessively pounding
My face got excited with my body that's unable to remain still
The longer I try to maintain my composer
It's an opportunity for my blood to circulate warmer
I got soften though I'm basically boiling within
My desirability is getting stronger by the sensitivity I'm feeling

Sympathetically connected, I am above the earth
My pulse beats to the drum of your chest during each and every breath
I'm definitely lost in those eagle's eyes in vain
And so connected that my body must be hidden under your skin
A miserable feeling to addict to
Something so sweet and an emotional to fall to
Thus, I find myself in a position so caring
Too late to recover because for you, deeply in love I'm falling

Kindness within

I strolled forlorn as a cloud
That drifted on high above the dale and hills
When all at one time I saw a crowd
A mass of brownish daffodils
Nearby the lake, below the trees
Quivering and skipping in the breeze

Despite the view, it's incessant as the stars that shine
Also sparkle on the Milky Way
They lingered in unbounded line
Down the outskirts of a bay
A large amount I spotted, at a glance
Chucking their heads in nimble dance

It is the representation of silent natives as they
Outshine the dazzling impression in glee
Living in their quarters made with clay
Providing, to each other, comfort and security
A population calm and splendid I thought
Passionate pleasure to my soul it had brought

From times to times, while on my chesterfield I lie
In available or in threatening mood
They visit my unflustered mind
That served as the synchronization of solitude
And afterward my kindness with contentment fills
Along with dances with the natives

Love to our Hero in Uniform

Completely a miracle is the creation of the universe
The resource of living being through the decayed as well
    as fresh
A place purely organized and protected by the mesosphere
Emerges the inhabitants of creation on such beautiful
    planet earth
Privileged by the Creator, we explore life with no fear
From the moment we exhale and enjoying the next breath
Is by the amplification of intelligence since the separation from the
    womb
To something still that we merely understood

Surprised we become to the numerous living impediments
That diminish our purpose thru what was once a blessing
Now challenged by our exploration of our own intelligence
Despite multiple layers of evolution, still we rely on the ones
    protecting
Highly spirited, and rich with devotion
I pledge to always be grateful for your bravery without limitation
Loved by me and/or perhaps by others
Will never balance your nature for the sense of humility
In hardship situations presented in places prosperous
    by terror
I declare my hearted affection with full sincerity

Your vocation offers the essence of giving with no return
To convey life to the vulnerable ones for a promising future
Through extreme pains you gain strength
Then one place to another, the world turns with your hard work in
    progress
Up high with ego carrying the fallen for the betterment of your fellow
    citizens

Content with pride your presence is gold to other's success
Clearly your heart pumps not for honor but a generation further
Hope for the poor with understanding of the world's successors

Because of you I stand, and understand the purpose of living
For you it's achievement as a role in life
But it's truly the frame of a hero wealthy with free-spirit
Many thanks God for your presence, comfortable by your charming
    kind
Without reflection, deeply I thank you
For your service in hard work, I look up to you
Dearly I love you in my weakness, fear, or a circumstance eerie
Blessing as you deliver is a keystone to humanity worldwide
Without you would exist a world absolutely silly
Your compensation is priceless and therefore, to the end I'll be by
    your side.

Men of Fatherhood

Half way up the mountain top
Find the city of Angels made of sky scrapers with dazzling lights at night
Looking south overlooks the volley with successful crops
From the hard work of men to a life that's right
An outstanding experience by the level of success
Carried by these strong, and honorable men
While united with purpose in the mind of greatness
Devoted to the future by the resources of the land

Within the beauty also lies true life by its original roots
Embedded in the community with the tenure of family values
The understanding of prosperity
Through the hard work of courageous spirits and responsibilities
A group of mind together teaching life by plain actions
Moving the city through sweat and internal affection
Though devoted to their work
As the lifeline of humanity and to strengthen others

With a mentality of greatness also follows dependability,
Fully committed to their duties including their companion
Men of pride, and with the heart without comparison
Also, a mind occupied that most likely has no room for idiocy
With their formation of such a strong bond
Empowered by relationship structured from a base
Reflected by physical strength as well as God's grace
Through respect and enthusiasm far beyond

By the rising of the sun along the road side street
Hundreds of little ones happily are on their way to school
Some accompanied by men as it makes perfect sense
With the backup traffic, life appears full and absolutely interesting

Uplifted are they to the hearts of their young talents
In the face of the city, morals and values seem to be a blessing
As strong characters favor a father figure for an existence bitter sweet
They lied down the path of example to a future above the moon

As the sun comes to rest beneath the city
Its beauty brighten to the resemblance of the stars of the galaxy
Together as family they shine in the eyes of their spouse
As they live happily and live between the lines.
Goofy with the kids and very romantic with their commitment
The types of brave men, who treasure from sacrifices as endorsement,
Who views respect and dignity as the backbone of a positive future.
A safe and a quietude setting that inherit quality without measure

Music to my ears

Like the arrival of the spring season, come excitement for the rejoice of existence
Having the ability to budge freely and enjoy a great weather is absolutely worthwhile
The botanic life is back to normal, fully green, and with life in abundance
Flying creatures are back occupying space while singing different forms of melody of life
With the sounds all together, but still distinctive in a sense very unique
When the adorable sound echoes, one usually catches full attention
One that brings joy to a level incredibly exclusive
From a living being currently in our life, with such an attractive qualification
From the driveway to the door, your voice brings a new shade to the moment
Just like a kid in its world, then back from work is your mother at the door
Your voice in my ears is energy in a form of contentment
By which I am lost, and become fully out of control

A character of yours stirs, and warms me up, which always gets me melted
A broad shoulder of yours to carry life completely weightless
Courage to be great even when problems are constipated
That gives me the sense of humility without ego but perhaps worthless
The boost to recover without condition but a gesture fully compulsory
A kind so absolutely rare, I would love your gene with someone to nurture
A nature of yours so adorable, that to me it's something to glory
Being with someone of your character is definitely my pleasure

Loving you not because you also do, but because it's what you demonstrate
You on the left side of my chest is enough for me to be soften
A moment in your affection is already much love to illustrate
Knowing you always there for me, is my bones collagen
Caring as you've shown is generally gentle
A type to admire and to lift you in aggressive confidence
Caring for you makes me docile and obviously humble
My mind is at ease because of the depth of your tolerance

Your presence is my daily nutrition
While your absence is rough and difficult to advance
Your enthusiasm is my coffee to start my vocation
Like a kid I am safe and fill with joy with you as my guidance
Your touch very smooth and soft but feel like a maven
Your way of communication is nothing but superb
Your attention is priceless but hard to understand
The way you care heals my pain like medicated herb

Around you I'm happy, and my day is bright
Knowing you is a grace and I'm glad that I'm blessed
Because your love is pure, I feel stunning and full of life
Your trust in me is spectacular and for which I feel modest
With you my world is a unique paradise
Thinking of you generates wisdom and redemption
The nature of your voice empowers and make me feel mobilized
While your affection is untainted and defined love as freedom

My dear Valentine

As you have been through love and you have been loved
I know for certain that you know pretty much the meaning of the word "Love"
To my own conception, love is undefined, but if it were possible to pick just three important
    key points of its definition, these three words would be
Affection 2) Trust 3) Honesty

Darling, if you were able to test my heart, it would show that I'm in love with you
That I already un-wrapped my heart to you
That every letter of the words that you've heard from me is from deep, deep, deep bottom
    of my heart
Mentioning your name and just a thought of you puts a charge in my heart.
But remember that is it impossible to be in love with someone if that special someone is not
    in love with you
Since I met you darling, my heart has been in a happy mood,
but you have something that is holding my love away from you.
Just a glance at your pics makes me believe that I am glancing at a comic book

Please tell me how to love you, to gain your honesty, and your trust.
Because I would love to be gentle and try never to be rough
My heart is damaging every time you fail to keep your promise.
That makes me doubt if I will ever be able to make you my princess
I know that love is blind, just the way that I am blind for you right now, and I am
    desperate not to see clear.
Don't let me get lost any further, tell me if I am on the right tract.
Please don't fake it, be real;
Since the expression of my feeling is nothing but straight facts.
If you don't love me, be strong
Don't let me stay around and waste my time
Tell me so I can move alone.
Thus, I won't have to get hurt any more times;

It doesn't really matter what the answer is, just be honest.

Speaking away from your heart is nothing to you but dishonest

If you chose NO as an answer, remember that the little piece of my heart that you already have (if you did) is never going to die.

But if you chose YES, then tell me that you love me and feel free to be my special valentine.

My exceptional mother

Beautiful is what you are
Grown and sexy in your full-fledged hips
Aged by experience and matured with swags
As you represent the feminine sex with beautiful tips
  As for me, you're the best
  And having you, I'm blessed
  My best way to thank you
  Is to tell you that I truly love you

Extraordinary is what you are
An outstanding provider
Even with or without a supporter
Who enjoys life even when the days got dark
  To my life, you're the access
  And having you, I'll reflect
  Thus, my best way to thank you
  Is to tell you that I truly love you

As weak as I am, I cause you pain every time I sin
But as the mother that you are, you offered ample time for change
While with love and patience, you showed kindness within
Which made you wiser and quite tolerant
  By your side, I'm free of stress
  Totally compassionate and not an actress
  Thus, my best way to thank you
  Is to tell you that I truly love you

During the traumatic times that I run to troubles
You were there and granted your best consolation
In the situation where I treated you so horrible
You warned me without asking a single question

From you, I experienced kindness
Through love and total respect
Thus, my best way to thank you
Is to tell you that I truly love you

Amazing is what you are
When I'm bored to death and my days are sad
You provided laughter
And in timeless moments you were my comfortable cheat-chatter
A nature of yours, is something to impress
And having you in my life is my ultimate asset
Thus, my best way to thank you
Is to tell you that I truly love you

A heartfelt super woman is what you are
Never restrained from my moments of need
Thus, spoiled I become by your generosity and charms
As you constantly push for greatness and success indeed
A woman truly without contest
In a character with cleverness
Thus, my best way to thank you
Is to tell you that I truly love you

My lifeline is what you are
Beautiful and great as you taught me thus far
You're everything that I am including what I stand
My light and your blood running through my veins
With your love I'll progress
And to you I promise
Thus, my best way to thank you
Is to tell you that I truly love you

Just a look at your brand
Makes me comprehend who I am
Fabulous you are I'm delighted you're my mother
One of a kind and the one I admire
          I Love you mother!!!

My ideal fancier

Special is my heart-beater
For being my love seeker
Whom with a character to admire
Who frequently fetches laughter
Who is exceptionally cleaver
Very optimistic and have little temper
Not a spectator but instead a great helper
One who hates being an accuser
But enjoys being my supporter
One who's far from a joker
But great investor in quality on all that does matter

With the experience of such a character
Also possesses the gentleness to acquire
One who dislikes a shout but prefers a whisper
Not treat me rough but instead like a feather
Not who detests me for being so disorder
Instead persuades me to be a magnificent organizer
Such a splendid innovator
That enhances my opportunity to prosper
The body of mine in your closer
Becomes my accurate thermometer
With all that I have encounter
I definitely become your number one admirer

Despite all the qualities to offer
Still plenty of features to aspire
As deeply as I envy your power
You are my explicit fearless soldier
The one who prefers the title of enforcer
Over the ideology of an imposer
The one who commits to hard worker
And focuses on establishing an umpire

One who gives up the title of a commander
To implement a method of new approach to be a protector
One who eliminates my terror
Who's definitely not a risk taker
One who's not my challenger,
But certainly my trouper
With you, I'll remain a fighter
As you'll always be my rescuer
Providing a milieu free of danger
Eases me with comfort to have you as my ideal shelter

No doubt; in my world, you are my consolidator
With the presence of yours, your patience is to master
Without any anger, comes ample room to conspire
Understanding and respect result matters smooth and tender
Knowing my vision to things I sequester,
The world must celebrate to a response sober
The One who Never tends to act like a rooster
Perhaps operates more like a good absorber

Yes with so much patience to gather,
Still presents with kindness to offer
The one I consider not a demoralizer
Instead is frequently my booster
One who never views me lower
But ready to raise me higher
One who definitely not a squeezer
But smoothes me like cocoa butter
Beside the quality of a good donor,
Also possesses the heart of a good producer
With much blessing received, I may not palter

So much for an obtainer,
For me, not much to provide as a replacer
As your kindness goes miles further,
You preserve much care to deliver

Thus, I become a good collector
Hoping one day I'll reflect better
With you, I'll remain never a complainer
Your mental strength with so much eager
I have to entirely recover
Your presence is my latter
That will make me an expander
When I was an encumber, you served as my scuba diver
When I feel in a cluster
You make me thinner and your sky scraper

Knowing how you care, as a receiver
It's as well a habit to consider
With a mind of a great competitor
Also shown the capability of a contemplator
Experiencing your ability as a great speaker
I'll manage to be a great thinker
To you I'm connected, and I refuse to sunder
The one who's always my restorer
And abandons the act of a disdainer
The one who use each opportunity to be a fantastic care giver
The one who's open minded and also a confessor
One who's not a good commentator
But a magnificent listener
Not a good criticizer,
But my number one reminder
My blood pressure drops with you as my leader
Peaceful with the record of a skilled settler
To me you are an integrator
And this makes me comfortable to have you as my primary liberator

Days young and old, my feeling has getting sharper
With your habit as a chaste demonstrator,
Your values increase with true love to offer
To whom I usher
Is the one my heart desire
Who is excluded among the cheaters
whom to my life is an adjuster
Who is not an imposter
But to whom I am a great believer
Who is an excellent kisser
As well as a great caresser
Whom is a great learner
As well as an excellent professor
One who loves to see me better
And with whom I feel spectacular
In the boiling summer you are my reefer
And my insulator during the terrible winter
You on my side make me twice smarter
With you, our path is absolutely brighter
Whom I cried for two days before Easter
Having you in my life is super
And to whom my affection will never expire
Therefore, you're unquestionably a keeper

My Lady

You are my Lady, the prettiest
Of the sky and the universe
Never have I seen anything better
To describe you any fewer

You are my Lady, charming and of course sweet
Whom without I'm crazy, sometimes freeze
Just to the idea of losing you
I would die, a word I much dislike and am fearful

You are my Lady, and I'm all yours
I give you all that I am including my endeavors
My hands, my voice, and my sights
My days, including my entire nights

You are my woman, the prettiest
I swear on my soul and the sky's best
That from every time I said
I love you is absolutely a feeling truly endless

You are my lady, you're the finest
To whom I recognize love the best
To the imperfection of our pain
In thousands of bouquets of poems

You are my lady, you're the sweetest
I love you in white and in velvet
I love you in the sexy pajamas of yours
I love you, and I love the bad manners of yours

You are my lady, the most endearing
The one I care for and share my feelings
You are my queen all year round
My love for you is quite pure and far beyond

My love in question

My love is of a nativity as rare
Since an article eccentric and high
It was begotten by despair
Upon unfeasibility in heights

Noble despair on your own
Could illustrate me so delightful a thing
Wherever shabby hope could near boast flown
Although unsuccessfully flapped its tinsel wing

Nonetheless I swiftly might arrive
Where my unadulterated character is fixed
But destiny does flatten wedges drive
And always crowds itself betwixt

For chance with indignant eye does see
Two faultless loves, nor lets them close
Their unification would her ruin be
Her tyrannical influence depose

For that reason her diktat of steel
We as the distant poles comprise placed
However love's whole world on us does wheel
Not by themselves to be embraced

Except the frivolous heaven fall
And earth a number of new paroxysm tear
And, us to adhere, the humanity should all
Be restricted into a mesosphere

When lines, so loves slanted may possibly well
Themselves in every angle greet
Excluding ours so truly parallel
Still endless, can never meet

Thus, the loves which do us bind,
But destiny so jealously debars,
Is the juxtaposition of the mind
As well as antagonism of the stars

Natural beauty

In the eyes of the beholder we find beauty
In the face of nature, it is far from diversity
Through the simplicity of life, beauty is natural
Through the attraction of its kind, it's sometimes inimical
By the study of individuality, it's explored by varied angles
Unique and settled and very untangled

To the make-up of its brand, it's the face as a passport
With different shape and forms that serve as vital support
With a glance at your class, your beauty is well reflected
With an anatomical feature plain and naked
Beauty as the eyes, clear and focus like an eagle
With full and lengthy lashes form such a great shadow
Cheeks fine and fleshy with such attractive dimples
Represent nature as a stunning example
Nose formally pointy and gently well elevated
As engineered from above not by physicians previously created

Beauty as you are, color is based on texture
The skin clear and plain compose such a magnificent fixture
Your lips curved and groovy shape the picture of a joyful raceme
Damply colored and comprise of the resemblance of a healthy stem
Hair so relaxed and simple,
But still reflects character in its inner circle
While kinky, straight, or curly hair preserve beauty very natural
Such an attractive feature matches with your head slightly oval
Absence of makeup and arts utterly amplify purity
Where plain and simple signify security

Beauty ignores sizes and shapes
As each has its own pride in a manner to accentuate
Length and width are ingredients to a polymer
Uniquely essential to a perfect posture

Beauty is natural not by visual perception
But by the formation of amazing composition
Beauty is not determined by visual appearance
Instead by profound energy in a texture with fragrance

Natural beauty is nothing more than plain natural
Where true beauty is internally reflected while impacted on the
    external
With a smile so bright, nature appears happily comfortable
With a denture that beautiful it must've been stolen from an Angel
Ears perfectly measured make me picture a cute lamb so little
With your nose perfectly structured, it's almost unbelievable
A smile like yours resembles yeast in bread that elevates the face
    and makes you lose visual
This brings joy with a smile of yours absolutely hysterical
You definitely have the smile to kill
thus, smiling at me just makes me ill

Beauty as adorable as it may appears,
Being natural is something to endear
Besides the appearance of beauty being so natural,
Character in addition is definitely exceptional
Open-minded and outgoing is certainly optional
While simple respect and understanding is complexly rational
With a nature of yours so humorous
With you I have a blast with every moment being nothing but
    hilarious
With such a beauty and character it must be a metaphor
To me your quality is impeccably something
    to die for
With all that's been said, "You are my natural beauty!!!"

Plain love

Captivating a quiet moment thinking of love by intensity
Of course by definition, it's self explanatory
Compared to an ephemeral obsession, it's rather a characteristic thoroughly eternal
Filled with aspiration but plain and simple
A straightforward sensation presented with kindness
That burns to the right moment totally effortless

To the extent of our knowledge, it's not a fabric of society
Intriguing for a cause is a ritual marking the length of our measure
Certainly contradictory to a gift by the Divine mercy
Suitable with such character is a bourse of treasure
A sensation without rules but includes with exception
That even with reason of dismay, it's a general feeling without omission

It's the motive of adoring through the act of caring
Taking initiative for the betterment of others
While engaging in tiny details that may seem worthless
But, build up to trust and confidence by the provision of shelter
It's the nature of good judgment with your existence countless
And taking refuge in the Lord's grace within

Despite the degree of our blunders, we still benefits the privilege of forgiving
As hard as it may appear, this is freedom
And to the level of this greatness, it's awesome
As in many phases, love is caring sometimes without the need of giving
It's an example that love requires unconditional respect
By trying to understand others and eager to be unwearied in all aspect

It's nearly possible to recall the number of times we did act generous
But absolutely unfeasible to recall the number of times we expect a quittance
Acknowledgeable as we all of it, this is not a proper act of munificence

A Heartfelt act of support by giving or helping mentally or bodily has no room for
    regrets
As in return, the reward will reflect
Thus, an action based on love without distinction is insidious

Showing affection with grief deserves no remuneration
While fulfilled with humor is a weapon very dangerous even without ammunition
True love requires no mood
It is rather entrenched in the character despite of the desire
Such natural feeling disregards the study of the moon
And carried on permanently such behavior merits the attention to aspire

Believing in the Almighty or not, his love is everlasting
Splendid is he even with our behavior still in question
Love from within does no generate by personal curiosity
Instead, embrace a situation as a moment of opportunity
As in return for our flaws, we owe gratitude with true admiration
Therefore, it is considered our duty to love each other regardless of our stings

Thankful to you

Like a moment of hunger and now minutes of a post-meal
I am fulfilled, thrilled and in a twinkle happily I feel
Like the substance of your essence, it's nothing for granted
An instant without your presence is nothing to play with
Like breaths per minutes compute rate of respiration
Also we take air for granted; without you I'm of annihilation

A smile from your farm, is organic to my health
Just like a rose of your kind does humble my flesh
As a stare at your globes
Is night light to my flaws
A thought from your cranial sachet
Is my vaunted works of Art I will no way forget

Since the sun disappears then come I missing the light
Then the day rises like your eyes in my mind
Like water in fruits to the grace of its roots
Come your presence in my life overcoming my native rout
Also like the omniscient spirit you judge quite well
To the quality that never fell

The work of your breed blossoms hope of a future near
And to the ire is the option of life with the extinction of fear
Without your support is life out of sort
As the appearance of my success felt your company aboard
Engaging in outstanding efforts, but sill broken I stand
With you as my ultimate posture is my upright skeleton

To you I recognize the degree of my existence
Well established by your concern and absolute tolerance
True to the heart as well as your quick action
I am blessed and tested by your undivided attention
Your love to my soul is on a permanent streak
That delineates true love as a two way street

I am who I am, hallowed by your toil of assurance
Robust and untamed, I'm flourished by perseverance
A quality of friendship plain and simple but exceedingly rare
But a champ of life well asserted with flamboyant flares
To the Ultimate force above I owe gratitude
From his blessing to you I've changed in magnitude
Life in your world is wonderful
Thus, to you I am absolutely thankful

The Art of Perfection

Beyond the empty space of the Universe
Only the divine High is able to see higher than the flying birds
Nothing can be more perfect than the arrangements of the planets
Who amongst us have the ability to think so deep? Not even a genius
Besides the visible creatures that can be seen
Why do we doubt and always tempting to sin?
Yes, it was created so enormously and perfect
That I can only imagine the time it happened in the tense of Past-perfect

Wow! . . . amazing as it is, a genius as He is
How the idea of keeping our location naked brings us sun rays
While covering it with a layer of atmospheric reaction brings us rain
How layers and layers of clouds can be so thin?
But trying to look through you won't see a thing
How do we get the knowledge of flying thousands of tons?
And Being in opposite ends of the world, we can still be engaged in close conversations

Because of all these miracles, I come to understand your beauty-ology
Because of the diversity of nature, that creates the ecology
Because of my interpretation of the book of Genesis
He had to be very sexist

How did you get to smile so bright?
While your teeth are so white
How did your skin get to be so brown?
While your eyes are also brown
How did you get so thick?
And be complimented with those cute cheeks

How your body gets to look so smooth
And still be presented with these sexy and bumpy grooves
How can you think so light?
And look so fly
In that sense you must be so smart
And to me, you really rock

How beautiful is your chin
And still have that beautiful skin
I can see the world in your eyes
When you look at me and smile
Looking at your nose
Make me wish I was a rose
Looking at your chest
Make me realize how much you're blessed
Pardon me, but thinking of your buttocks
Would make me feel worse
Looking at your ears
Make me feel weird
But seriously, just a glance at your Lips
Is enough to make me feel weak

If he wasn't sexist
He would not create us on day six
As being said, we must have been created on the last day out of stress and exhaustion
While you must have been created fresh on day one with perfection

To my knowledge, your beauty has no limit
You're so perfect that there's no room for critics
To my description
Your perfection is without distinction and competition.
Therefore; you are my Art of Perfection!!

·

The Color of love

It is very simple that love has only one color which is of course "black"
Do you agree? Whatever . . . I can read your filthy brains from far
Well, the color definitely has to be "white"
As we all should agree, if you believe me then you must be a psyche
To be factual, it is not any specific color from the rainbow
Perhaps the sweet colors of skittles

Instead, it is all the colors as a combination
As been said, it is the insight of one's own eye conception
Won't you agree that this makes such better sense?
If that's so, what would you say for the ones who are missing that sense?

If you think about the above,
Maybe a blind is incapable of love
Better yet, we tend to believe that love is from the heart
Therefore, because of our blood, RED is the shade of the heart

Furthermore, the presence of blood is the sign of pain, something terrible, or a terror
If that is true, we should then concur that love has no color
For those who insist, if love is white
Which we use to remember the dead then, love has no life.
If we say that love is black
As black is the redden of absence of life, infinity and hardship, yet love is not right
If the color is black & white
Then Love has to be tough and without hope of life
If love is red
Then it is the sign of life as well as the problems that we everyday bled
If love is yellow
Then it is the color of the transition of life as dyeing leaves turn red and black after it had become yellow

To expire the debate on its color, love is instead invisible
While possessing strength and an attachment so irresistible
It is the sensitivity of an inner emotion that has no possibility to be dissected
It is the behavior of a burning affection that is definitely well reflected
It is the tiny existence in our heart that is not even capable of microscopically detected
While is it bulky enough to be globally affected

It is the feeling of giving in without resistance
While carrying a behavior with consistence
It is not a moment chosen with a certain degree of affection
But a moment that exists with absolutely no selection
When love is well defined
It has no potential to follow in a fine line
As the measure of love is inexplicable
It is also implausible

True love is the acceptance of a package with nothing in mind
And completely engage with the inner passion fully blind
True love does not have the appearance of any coloration
Perhaps reflected by its behavior and its consistent reaction
With all that's being said to describe love, if you still have a color in mind
Then love definitely has to be blind!!!

The eyes of a shotgun

All the way down beneath the skies
I come to find my angel by the oaks and pines
Blended with the colors on the ground
But reflected by the sun is the shaft of light from her gown

Deeply focus on the magnificent scenery
My attention is guided to nothing but the face
Hardly able to make that up, and to which I lost gravity
I stare so much that without looking I tied the right of my shoe lace

Wow! With the background behind
She brings beauty to the landscape
A face so smooth and fine
This utterly designs nature with me out of place

With the valley in full spring
Her jewelries merge with the splendid flowers
The ones that reveal her face by such a beautiful texture
Accompanied with a smile that brings joy at a hint

Her hair twisted and laid on and the back of the shoulder
Gives the vision of the Amazon in mid summer
Something to strongly admire
While I wonder if it's perhaps time for my coiffeur

Staring at her big and round eyes
Added on her hair style that messes with the flesh of my heart
Therefore, in her eyes I would rather die
Knowing that she'll always be my guardian seraph

The great of soul in the winter

From left to right, and through the horizon
Spectacular it is for a beautiful day of winter
Unified in a color by a thick snow white,
Then, in the parking or along the street all vehicles were gone.
And large flakes of fresh snowfall repainting all over my heavy
   sweater,
And my boots are two feet below with my blood turning white

Despite the lack of color
I'm then fascinated by the storm being so beautiful.
As I walked down the street, at least where I believe is the
   street
I stumbled on things up and down or
Between objects I go up and down, but thanks to my black
   boots
That I managed to cover a few blocks on my two frozen feet

The more I advanced, the view gets extra spectacular
I'm approaching a sound that's nothing like a vehicle
Excited by the noise, and contemplated by the beautiful day
I run down the slop, and below is a flat surface where many kids
   are.
They were skating in round on the snow with much ice below
I got warmed up with thrill though I was covered with snow
   flakes

As I jumped into the crowd, I ended up on the right
No one seemed to mind and they decided to start fresh
But as I swung in motion, my feet got hefty and felt very thick
Ashamed then I felt; I stepped aside and watched how everyone
   is unified

On their snow white ice skates going in circle from right to left
Unhappy at the moment thus, it's my fault so I faced it

With the decision to rush back home, I made my single steps for
 two
Avoiding the distance, I went straight through the parking
Where no path was clear as the snow covered it all
Then I heard a weak noise in a hole that the lot is next to
As I looked down the ditch, there was someone twisting and
 turning
A six years old boy lying down face up, freezing, and covered
 with snowfalls

Rushing to the rescue, I grabbed him and barely able to lift him
 then,
In the parking lot I took him and dust off the snow he was freezing
 of,
Covered with my sweater and roughly carried him on my shoulder
 that's fairly large
As I walked down the street, my neighbor rushed to my rescue
 and,
Run to his house where he laid him down and wonder how long
 he was there for
Then, grateful I felt saving someone on this winter day so
 spectacular

The "L" in Loving

From biblical verses to our love of humanity "Love" is what it's said to be . . .
"L O V E".
From friendships to friendships, family to family, intimacy to lovers, we hear often in
different form of phrases the word that we love.
From times to times we hear us contradicting ourselves misinterpreting the meaning of true
love.
Women tend to convince men that even if they express the word they do not know what
they are talking about.
Over and over when kids use the word, we accuse them for not knowing what it's all
about.

Men have the habit of saying that love is not real
But after committing a mistake, they wish that only pronouncing the word could heal.
L O V E, as simple as it is, as self defined as it is, as many times as we hear it,
Or as many times we feel good to hear it, to what does really "Love" simplify?
The confusion is clear, but it is a combination of actions and feelings of its true impact that
we can describe.

Love . . . is the action of adoring someone or something or what you believe in.
Love . . . is the feeling of affection for someone or by someone of with you are dealing
Love . . . is worshiping someone you trust in
Love . . . is the devotion to go after your true inner feeling toward someone or something
Love . . . is caring for someone or something you cherish
Is showing hearted feelings for someone you except in your life or something you work
hard for on a regular basis
Love . . . is the irresistible bond built up toward someone or something that unable you to
detach yourself from.
Love . . . is the commitment to accept someone's flaws and imperfections to create the art
of a union.
Love . . . is the combination of trust, confidence, understanding, and happiness with someone
without condition.
But why do we tend to formulate our own definition?

Due to changes in society and evolution from generation, its true meaning remains the same.

We apt to lose the meaning of love based on our own needs, and to which we look to blame

Our understanding of love can be a mystery

But most of the times we tend to be insensitive, and often a bit self-satisfactory

In many occasions, we tend to love with a lot of expectations

Which usually blocks the path of continuous affection

Love is neither ugly nor pretty

Perhaps it has no trend of beauty

Love has no features

Instead full of respect

Love deeply has no character

To tell you the truth, its calculated value is priceless

The smile . . .

As the world was created in the midst of multiple inequalities,
Yet everything has its own beauty
In many occasions, the splendor of the world's creatures is thus a mystery.
It's unfortunate that we reside on the same planet
But communicate in different manner
Maybe not so dreadful since that gives us the ability to identify our disparity
   in culture

We learned different classes of animals to their divisions and groups,
But, understanding their way of information from one to another is off the
   hook
Yet, as we're genetically the most unique being on this planet, culture still
   takes us apart
Not behaving alike, in many occasions race differences set obstacles in our
   path
Observing each animal grouping including the human race, we have one thing
   in common
Depicting that common message or behavior, we know happiness in full
   blown

To our humanity, beauty is a luxury
While happiness is a virtue of liberty
Besides every things that we adore from one another,
There is one thing that can use to convey in a most powerful manner
Besides everything we accept to describe a person's exquisiteness
No shapes, or curves, or other features can distinguish it in its best

Throughout the world, we recognize the elemental nature of happiness in its
    kind
And that transmits enormously in your smile
A smile of surrendering,
In a moment thoughtless with complete lack of pressure
Free, and something truly unquestioning
One that pictures love without any measure

A smile that speaks the truth
Totally transforms the face to a goof
One that expresses understanding
Full of life and very authentic
In a gesture very engaging,
Confident, and incredibly fantastic

A smile perhaps from someone unhappy
But one that articulates your contentment with me
One that deforms your face to an angel
Shining so bright, it's marvelous
And with your eyes lost between your cheeks to a character so adorable
You bring hope through a smile so beautiful

A smile that reveals all the existing muscles on a human's face
Disturbing the laws of physics by facial grimace
One that brings the color of your cheeks to the most loving colors of the
    rainbow
One that brings admiration to your face full of happiness
And one that makes me grasp that your lips does comprise muscles
While your chin lost its structure with softness

A smile that makes your ears dance
One that enables me to appreciate your existence
One that makes me realize the depth of your dimples
And the one that crafts me truly humble

Jhonny B. Pierre

A smile that makes you blind because your eyes went under
With a joyful frown that barriers your flaws over
One that causes me to blush just by looking at you
And opens my heart to a feeling without a clue

A smile that expresses security around me
One that depicts your nature effusively in love
One that embraces the ideology of the right therapy for the world
One without a doubt reads your friendship with loyalty

A smile that melts to the degree that I should care for you
One who loves without condition
In a promise implanted in speculation
One that optimistically views life in a good mood

A smile obviously from the heart
Appearing in a simple smile of comfort
which forces my heart to a moment of a silent flirt
Enlightening a world of mine so dark

To my Eyes . . . .

*Fortunately I happen to have 20/20 eye site

*Not only do I have clear vision, but you damn right I can see very bright

*So when I tell you what I see

*I hope you don't hesitate but believe in me

*Therefore, to my eyes . . . I see real dark chocolate among the fake ones

*the only way you can be so smooth, and black you have to be an African one.

*To my eyes . . . only an African race can be so fine and fly

*Therefore, when I say you're fine, I can't be any more right

*To my eyes . . . I've seeing it all

*And I can truly say that you have it all

*To my eyes . . . you are created without any error

*Your body shape is so perfect; your mom must had pushed you out without
   any pressure.

*Look at your eyes, they are so beautiful; I'm already melting by just staring
   at them

*And your nose is so well placed on your face, God must had checked a few
   more times after created them.

*To my eyes . . . only looking at your chicks put a smile on my face

*And your chin couldn't match any better with your face.

*To my eyes . . . your ears are so cute,

*As I can't see mine, I wonder if they are also that cute.

*Girl, your lips . . . really to my eyes . . . no words can describe the round curve,
   the pink color, and . . . damn!!!

*I better close my mouth before I start dribbling . . .

*Just thinking of you sometimes makes me feel like I am dreaming

*I have seeing many women, different types of women, women with different
   style, different heights, but telling you the truth, to my eyes . . . I never
   have seen a woman like you.

*That only is enough to make me go kookoo . . .

The way you talk, walk, laugh, smile and look at me always make me wish I could replay it in slow motion.

To my eyes . . . when I think of you, I have full belief and understanding of you with full intuition.

To my eyes . . . you are so unique and indistinctive, thinking only that you exist gives me hope to live life in full introspection.

To my eyes . . . the definition of happiness is with you as my completion

To my eyes . . . a woman like you is what a real man need.

To my eyes . . . a quick look at you and knowing that you care for me is my number one medicine.

Only hearing you saying my name makes me feel humble and docile.

Sweetie, having a chance to touch you does cure my problems,

With a chance to hug you makes me feel soft but also feel like a maven,

Having a chance to rub your feet would make me feel the chemistry of your skin,

Having a chance to play with your arms by pulling its hairs gives me a sense of integrity,

Having a chance to rub your back and your neck would make me lose my pulse,

Having a chance to look and feel every curve of your body would make me fully understand that from God's work you are a masterpiece,

Having a chance to touch your face, look at you in the eyes, fixing your eyelashes would give me the humility to be yours and nowhere close to be a hoodlum,

Having a chance to feel your chin and to smoothly and softly touch your lips and place my lips on the pink and moist lips of yours would rupture the blood off my veins,

And bbllll . . . . I need to stop because it already gives me goose bumps.

Only thinking of you makes me feel weak.

Knowing a day that you're not doing well makes me feel sick.

Baby, to my eyes . . . you are definitely my point of life.

To my eyes . . . you signify, clarify, modify, amplify, beautify, qualify, and simplify my life.

Therefore, to my eyes . . . with everything that I am or may not be, I would need nothing but you to be mine.

To my eyes . . . you are a real black princess for life

To my eyes . . . perhaps if you grant me a chance, I can be your prince alive.

Tolerance

Lesson from other species, it is the duty of the skilled to facilitate the inexperienced
While patience through repetition taught us true coaching values
Similarly the toddler as I was, my action was gullible and made completely no sense
Dull as I was, my innocence was rather funny occurring by handfuls

Years go by then my inner feelings have revealed through other's care
Eventually blessed I became, then I cultured reality which I dare
In the course of life comes the understanding of right and wrong
Embedded in nature's affection, I am the product of character full of compassion

Love is blind, but speaks a language moderately loud
Very focused and alive, there's no room for malicious discovery
As time elapsed then appeared my decision in a heart-throb
Where on my own life is a fantasy

Through the youth of the existence of mine
Error is a virtue with a reality simply blind
An approach rejected and sheltered with shame
Whilst the chance of coping is rather viewed nowhere sane

Analyzed or judged, still categorized as an abuser
As by thee I'm not judged is relevant to my existence
Forgiving by selection denotes a judgment indeed wiser
Thus, by example I surrender and grant another chance

Arrogance in your make-up as a dominant genotype
Reflects a behavior of mine like of an inclusive genocide
Egotistic and boorish with improper etiquette
Is considered a character similar to mine as I'm also imperfect

Contemptible adding to the lack of appeal masters beauty to its minimum
While living with such disposition requires the proper resolution
To embrace the attractive natures and to neglect the others by a lump sum
Result in contemplating my happiness around the ones that nourish my attraction

Despite your differences come room for my complicatedness
Bearing with me generates a supple heart with tenderness
To which I gain courage with a world of tolerance
To comprehend your beauty through massive defiance

From toddler to presence, perfect I will never be
Judging in opposite side only reflects comparison of us both
Acceptance is highly a merit to what living should be
Which consequently an experience to valuate as my ultimate mythologue

Why does it hurt?

Thanks to the most High for my striking existence
And knowing someone like you is my everyday strength
The unique style of yours is nothing but incredible
And a beauty like yours is seriously unimaginable
Well maintained with fragrance
While only an angel can compete with such an appearance

Crazy as I may well be
It's also accurate how my love is real
You I desire
Cause your look is my fire
To a nature so splendid that I picture my future
Charming and docile wedge the excuse for forfeiture

A heart full of promises is benevolent to you
With all that I am, my soul will surrender soon
Obviously, you are my hot chocolate in the winter
My electricity running through my house meter
Also the ginger in my caffeinated tea
As well as the sugar in my dark coffee

Despite the confidence I have in you, it hurts
To the degree of my admiration toward you, it hurts
With the affection burning inside me, it hurts
Having so much respect to endear, it hurts
Imagine with you how my life would be full, it hurts
You that I may not endure happiness without, but why does it hurts

Being on my mind constantly, it hurts
Sitting next to me at the bus stop waiting patiently, it hurts
On the dining table across each other, it hurts
In the shower as my back rubber, it hurts
On the sofa as my head rest, it hurts
With these positive hallucinations I fetch, why does it hurt?

Acknowledging the need of you each day next to me, it hurts
Then having you rejecting me, it hurts
Experiencing you becoming so disrespectful, it hurts
Misunderstanding by such magnitude, it hurts
Every time you give me no attention, it hurts
If that's what it takes in consideration, then why does it hurt?

To the crest that our warmth has lost its course, it hurts
Speaking without you listening, of course it hurts
Unable to speak without a good scream, it hurts
Doubting the odds of you cheating, it hurts
Thinking of the family we could build together, it hurts
Acknowledging that love is a venture, and requires a good gambler, then why
*   does it hurt?*

With such a great deal of love to offer
Perhaps I went too far in the future
The more I feel in love
More patience is required from above
A feeling without rush and with reactions so gentle
If Love must be so calm and simple, then why does it hurt?